Titles by *Langaa* RPCIG

MAP

Musings On Ars Poetica

Poetic Reflections on the Poet and Poetry in Verse

Bill F. Ndi

Langaa Research & Publishing CIG
Mankon, Bamenda

Publisher:
Langaa RPCIG
(Langaa Research & Publishing Common Initiative Group)
P.O. Box 902 Mankon
Bamenda
North West Region
Cameroon
Langaagrp@gmail.com
www.langaapublisher.com

Distributed outside N. America by African Books Collective
orders@africanbookscollective.com
www.africanbookscollective.com

Distributed in N. America by Michigan State University
Press
msupress@msu.edu
www.msupress.msu.edu

ISBN: 9956-558-43-5

DISCLAIMER

This is a work of fiction. Names, characters, places, and incidents are either the author's invention or they are used fictitiously. Any resemblance to actual places and persons, living or dead, events, or locales is coincidental.

Contents

Dedication

To my Late Father, Stephen Fohndung NDI and to my Late Maternal Grandmother, Lydia Liba'ah. These two wonderful beings both shaped my visions of the world in many ways and still serve as my muse to the practise of this wonderful art. They are never far away!

Bill F. NDI

Author's Note

When I set out writing poetry while in high school, my goal was just to write for my fellow classmates. That was my target audience. Not quite ambitious. However it extended to the Cameroonian audience and African audience and the globe trotting me imposed a target not limited in scope: geographical, political, economical, social, racial or linguistic. This last mention will obviously have monolinguals laughing or smirking wondering how poems written in English could target any audience, French or Hispanic. And the poet responds with his enjoyment of Cuban music without any understanding of Spanish as well as his enjoyment of Mozart without any knowledge of German. The magic of poetry and that of music is as complex and simple as life in itself and when humans stop complicating it for themselves so does poetry like life become everybody's domain. It is the domain of the universe inspired by it and produced for all in the universe.

Most of the poems in this collection were originally intended for different collections in which they still maintain their places. The thought of putting this collection together was actually born of a discussion with one of my students, a poetry enthusiast by name Caroline Hoang Minh Phuc who after reading "The Way To Go" approached me with a series of questions on the roles and functions of a poet and his art as was in the past and is in the present. I thought a brilliant way to answer her question as well as the questions many a poetry lover would ask even after reading Wordsworth and Coleridge, was to put together poems I have written on this subject, with an eventual intention of collecting poems from other writers in the same vein. However, scavenging through my works I found what now constitute *Musings on Ars Poetica: Reflections on Poets and Poetry in Verse.*

As a practising poet, my vision of the poet, his art, be them of the past, i.e. my predecessors' and/or those of future poets, constitute the essential ingredients of the reflections in this collection I would like to sum in these lines below:

My soul in this work as a poet I place
And hope in your hearts it does find a place
Minds of poets my portrayal
With hopes none sees betrayal
On the highway to the poet's psyche
In his journey through societal psyche.

My contention here is that the poet has the rare gift of slipping into the self and psyche of his society to empty the dark depths where the treasures of burden and sadness are hidden. He empties and exposes to the world to see even personal repression of feelings by far outweighs those imposed throughout History by tyrants. It is above all, his greatest task of filling these depths with the joys and expectations of the society. This objective stance by the poet places him above the fanatic whose subjectivity pushes the world adrift and makes of the poet a universal man of peace.

Poetry is and should be an outlet to document personal/ universal convictions, experiences and observations no matter how controversial or taboo they may be, most especially in the face of great wrong, unfairness and brutality. Take pleasure riding on this straight and crooked road.

Bill F. NDI

Acknowledgement

The author would like to seize this opportunity to express from the depth of his heart, sincere gratitude to all those whose moral and/or material support did somehow warrant the present work to see the light. I would like to start with she who is dearest to me, Dr Yaya Fonye Odette NDI, my German twin brother, Uwe Terton and family, Dr Uche Menakaya and family. Special thanks to Mohamed Ali for his passion and love for poetry. I can't forget him coming to my office everyday, after hours for a reading and appreciation session. The list of those to thank is long and inexhaustible for many people had me positively in the prayers. And to them all I say, Thank you all!

Bill F. NDI

The Way To Go

Parents envisioned education
And told us
They saw him home coming with the best dividend
And dreamily still we did
Ope our ears wide
Like antelopes theirs when danger sensed,
Hoping schooling issues bread winning ticket!

So we started up with education
So did we realise writing
Could be the ticket itself
And to writing we took

What We Do,　　　　　# What They Do

Holding onto nothing
Watching the state falling
In a bottomless pit
To the brim filled with shit
Tricking the poor they choose
For they're the golden goose
To slave and fetch their gold
That will project them bold
To those that espouse wealth
The sole backer of health.

Holding on to poetry
Looking at a country
So shattered, in a world
Shattered that not a word
Can trick her together
Choose wisdom and gather
The pieces to make a belle
And invite a wedding bell
From them that in poetry
See a pack of misery.

Consistency

Poets' longing is not contradiction free
Nor is their art from novel uses free!
Someday somewhere, if you see a poetic scape
Of these void, gladly I'd show you an escape
Rivers use to flow back to their sources
And have carts pull their horses
And would even be stunned to see a show
One of an active peaceful volcano.

Some of the Best

They must be some of the best
And would be proved the deadliest
For atop the pyramid they're sharp
Pointing edge of the spear of mishap

Afoot pyramid we the brunt bear
Hoping a common front shall them tear
Were our foundations not for this strong
We'd for shit-o-cracy sing a song

A song we would not from our lips
Come this danger to minds like slips
To them that themselves the best see
We must not weaken our tsunami.

Talking and Hearing

Far from my talking
None but my hearing
Does beat the drum
Sound bomb, the bump!
Sticking in the heart
Of this power drunkard
Yet, caressing those of my kind
Dying for the drunk to be kind
Listen and listen to my hearing!
Ignore and ignore their lordly ring.

Eee After Vee

Free yourself from evil
Displace eee after vee
And expect not in your platter veal
But a shroud around you, a veil
Holier than thou
You would not doubt
The eee outside veil
Brings in the devil
Either way
That's the sway
Vile
Evil
Prick him with eee in
Peace you'd know within
The thorny face of the universe
Long abandoned in poets' unique verse.

4

Poets' Pen Prick

The poet gets up in the morning
Without blanket, mourning
The sweet, sweet dreams of last knight
Whose apparel braved the night
Mare above him did linger
Asking he points a finger
At monsters finding pleasure
Depleting human treasure
With the finger he should a pen pick
With which pen our hearts he should prick
Then up we shall sit and see unveil
Before our eyes devils we did hail;
To the poet's pen prick, respond, respond
And in your world like fish in a pond
Without strain swim, swim, swim
Not 'twixt sea and imp swing
But to single freedom fly
And baby-like in a cod lie.

Big Bags With Lust Full

With truths full
Poets aren't fools
Were they to tell you you were beautiful
In them you will see big bags with lust full
With no sense of striving to be wealthy
With ink to scribble these words of beauty
The risk they take as they would with shit
Smear and drag horrid creed down a pit
Cleansing our world with their pen
And like Daniel in the den
Of lions who thirst after street man's flesh,
Scrape skies and lick arses all afresh
Longing for plebeians to lick their boots
Turning eyes blind as they carry loots;
Blind, poets won't be blind
With Milton will dine
On bread crumbs blindness has in hearts' eyes
That'll look at frozen hearts and melt ice
Big bags with lust full
Poets would were not fools.

Sharp Thorny Pen

Transforming my pen into a thorn
   I pricked the paper hard
And it squirmed and squirmed hard
   For all to find the magic horn

    Magic horn
    Magic horn
   Let flow the tune of life
   Let flow the food of life

Show how we do dance of the soul
Show how we make gift to the dole

   Visa a check to the bad mate
   Visa the dirge to come on skate
   Sharp thorny pen hit really hard
   Till we see the fall of the old lad

Fall on the spot
Making lives sport
When the dirge shows up on a skate
So he can see what it means: hate…!

Tend to the King's Ear

The place was Frankston
On two occasions
The trail was Baxter
The songbird, butcher
Would chop my ear
And reckon I hear
What on earth I don't know
And I quest if he does know

> Our kings need theirs pulled
> So they can help pull

Us out of this quagmire
One in which we perspire
And I ask why on earth
He should my ear unearth
When in this mire the brunt of thorns we bear
   With a monarch forcing this smile we wear
To tell the world his smelly shit's of perfume made
   And the world I implore to have this in state laid
So, go pull the king's ear butcher bird
For him to hear babies cry at birth.

Put not Asunder

In this nation, so divided
Why should we be separated?

Were poets' mission to put asunder
Then together we won't gather
Here under this old baobab tree
Allowing us all to freely sing for free.

Its thornless bark
Attracts no bark
And on him we gladly lean
Letting our joys to be seen
Big old baobab tree
Needing no count to three

For joys to explode like flames
Surprising kings in their games
Burning and burning our health
In their raging madness for wealth…!

My Clean Hands

Give me our king to kill
I'd just take him up hill
From where he could see
The crown of misery
He has birthed all his reign
Washing our hopes down the drain
Much more like him
Monster from film
Not my hands,   I won't dip in blood
Would his conscience through his tears wrought
The flood to sweep him and his away
To keep our thorny misery at bay

Back to Sender

Baldhead beheaded
Walking barefooted

On a thorn did step
Looked round and the day cursed

A pat on his back said
"Not the day but the king
"He is far from being dead
"And in your pain has a fling
"Orgasmic throes throw him
"And with joy he does beam.
"So show the crazy bald head
"The sick he has infected
"If he won't come out of his mansion
"Naked the ills outside that mansion."
Beheaded baldhead went forward
Singing "Coward"
And the king stepped backward
Screaming "reward"

Frail and Strong

Poor little Anglophone, gleefully sing a song
How mad brother francophone won't see you bone strong
Fear not to deride that unfriendly thorn
He on your crawling path put when you're born
Now seen from head to toe
As always he won't slow
His mad spree of power hunger
Sing your song, let it last longer
Aspire not after his deeds
Turn treasure page off misdeeds.
That will make a sane mind
Benefit humankind
Frail Anglophone strong
Sugary strong each thong
In their dream would want to kiss
Just as this same day
Recalling mayday
The nation showers with bliss

Bangolan Question

Before they brought us their school
Ghana had the Golden Stool
In their school they pointed towards Greece
Reducing us to what they did please
Telling us of the wild beasts,
Our ancestors with the least
Worry being the love for wisdom
Waiting to hear of a Greek kingdom
They never in mind had but were happy
Not without their own philosophy
As my father told me of his father
Who named my late uncle *Mundaka*?
A question in Bangolan
That for years did serve as scan
To rid the country of its thorns
And provide the nation with corns
With ucopia
Not utopia.

Mundaka translates "What have I done?"
Not the flat western "What have I done?"
But that which seeks to answer why
Spears, arrows and thorns seek not the sky
But fly after human hearts
In need of shields against darts
From nature and from our headmen
Worse than the goads of herdsmen
On the cows falling herding them down stream
As our headmen would rather see us scream
With their new song of Globalisation
Forgetting we would ours on compassion
As they their agenda make political
We of our agenda do make ethical
Ours and theirs might not be close
But fairness by the right dose
Forebears had in that primitive village
Not the global resounding with pillage.

Not Sweets

On my backward journey
Counting after forty
I try not to think
Of the thorns that pricked
And still do prick me
But would to be free
Fight
&
Fight
Like a cactus in the heart of a desert
Telling everyone it is not a dessert;
Easy food
From fast food
To be swallowed fast
By these crude outcasts
Seeing in their fellow humans sweets
Neither humans nor state are sweets.

Thorny Forebear

Nat Hawthorn his forebear
Did thread nakedly bare

Courage to be greeted from a seer
Were he not, he'd have embraced the rear
And savoured the thorn his forebear was
In the flesh of peace loving Quakers
Misdeed he called the witch hunt
At home witches we don't hunt
   The royalty run the show,
At will will make rivers flow
Yet, at will would hoard our wants
And mute we'd be not, let's chant!

Ants

Chant
To see the thorn out
And all thorns wiped out.

Thinking of High (Rivalry)

When we will have been dead and gone
Those who in us did see a thorn
Will sit back not without a sigh
Though they had thoughts they would be high
With us gone with their gun salute
Now they long for the music flute
Like dross once treated and berated
In our tombs from cries liberated
In their joys incarcerated
We would their larynx vibrated
With the music of regret
Far from a cattle egret
Pecking on the arse
Keeping clean our cows
Let herdsman remember
This family member
With cow and egret
There is no regret
For life moves on
With daily pun.

Of the Good Shepherd

A slap on the face loose
Look at the span
Think while you can
Before becoming shoes
For Alzheimer
Or dementia
To slip into you
And having you
Think not of the thorn
He does make you borne
You for his feet his shoes
Him for your head the booze
You who with words would slit
His throat, make of him shit
Now, you must think and leave a trace
A trace to graze the thought you raze
Wondering what pricked the head
We once viewed as good shepherd
Before handing him the goad
With which he treats us as goats.

No Cheating Lane

Gnashing their teeth
Seeing all the filth
Behind left by the King
Angry clouds did one thing

Spewing on poets roof
Hail as palpable proof
To the music drummed as they fall
For poets to bring down the big wall

Behind which like lions' mane
Kings would stray off the lane
By ignoring we defined it
Lane on which none should cheat

And if done
Would strike dawn
For poets to drive home this music
That like hawthorn does prick the sick

Their conscience purified
With none left petrified
Angry clouds gnash your teeth
For us to the sword sheathe

And spare ourselves these beings
 Whose presence trouble rings
With just the wrath of your hail
  We look up to for our bail.

Just The Bun King

Ask our rulers to run
Not towards us
Miles away with their thorn
They would make pus
They in their high office
Use against the masses

Their stomachs with quininegar full
Touch they've lost with being thoughtful
With that base drum size tummy
Sightless to see their mummy
When greeted by the welcomed hand
Shake from death that will on them land

With our cheers from high office they should run
Not only at the sound blasts of a gun
Applauded by the silence of thunder
Transporting with them the strange danger
With which rulers glory to see distress
Leaving just deflation as choice to press.

One & Only Number One

Cry we must not to say were in pain
Our towns our tears must not flood in vain
Laugh we cannot to say we are happy
Of our towns your laugh shan't make a mockery

You are number one to stick out like a thorn
On a rose or the horn on a unicorn
Which as children we did fancy
From storey building books at sea

Look around and read on faces
Soreness the billboard fun graces
Sunset stretching unend agony
Into the night we don't find funny

Laugh we cannot to say we are happy
Of our towns your laugh shan't make a mockery
Cry we must not to say were in pain
Our towns our tears must not flood in vain

Claiming you are father of this nation
Do that which will invite an ovation
With smiles on faces retrieving lost bliss
You buried silencing anything hiss

Cry we must not to say were in pain
Our towns our tears must not flood in vain
Laugh we cannot to say we are happy
Of our towns your laugh shan't make a mockery

Giving our nation a kiss on the lip
To leaving her with badly broken hip
You would we cried out our brain
For you leaving us in pain

Steel Sensitive

When society hurts so does a poet
Far from the truth with our crazy baldhead
With us at joy sad is crazy baldhead
This does not hold true for a mad poet

Who in his death is steel sensitive
When by the world treated as illusive
For being so touched seeing others touched
By this elf joying at the world scotched

Making plain poets true love for words
Scolding elf's hate stroke without words;
The battle twixt sword and pen
The poet does his resharpen

To stick in the flesh of the sword
Sharp to slay man matching not word
The penman would use to caress Hearts
The sword holding man would shoot with darts.

Boy/Speaker

In this house
Is a mouse!

That's true!
That's true!

Speaker!
Speaker!

I wish to know just one thing!
Can you tell me such a thing?

Yes Boy!
Yes Boy!

How wicked is our crown?
And why don't you frown?

He is the devil's incarnate!
That says why we can't demonstrate
For he holds a big grenade
That is not pomegranate.

What will happen if you did?

Our thorny crown will prick deep!

Isn't this reason to be our saviour?

You're Right! He'd make me his gardens manure!

The Journey

Writers might start off poor
Poor they are not, they pour
Their wealth in the heart of Art
Rich in beauty touching hearts

Writers wont money choose
To happiness refuse
By preference for money
Thorn pricking happy story

Man and woman the world may tell
With the conviction of Bill Tell
Who in this cradle love found
To his enemies dumbfound

Writers crave the world of old
Not the human world of gold
Calling their world primitive
In theirs that is deceptive.

Dream On! We'll Be Loyal

Speaking ex-cathedra

Our lords would beat us loyal
We only laugh at their dreams
Not until truth our ships breams
Our loyalty to end their royalty
Will beat its drum of sincerity
Just as we would beat our drums torn
When lords for their lies become thorns
If not, let them dream we'll be loyal
We won't yield showing their betrayal
For when we did enthrone them, all they pledged
Stood miles away from lies they swore to dredge
And today their dreams to coerce
We would transport in their hearse
And would stir shit to rock their thrones
With no chance of them birthing clones.

Ring Till They Fly

They do prick us with their thorns
We shame them by blowing horns
Now they are wringing us dry
Our bells must ring till they fly
With their cruise they pull a stunt
With our spears we shall them hunt
The art to tongue twist they have learned
As for long freedom we have yearned

And when they shall stop their tongue
The gates of their forts we'll throng
If they do not change their stance
Then we must hug resistance
Till their show comes to the end
For we're straight and must not bend
It is our planetary tapestry
Not just on it they sit on the tree
Lovely tree cleanse our world of emission
They make their sole polluting contribution
Not just to atmosphere
But so our art must not fare
And our bells shall only stop ringing
When our freedom they shall sop hoarding
If not ring and ring till they fly
Duty to which the must comply.

Spiky Hirsute

Short not of ink
Without a drink
Saying no words
Cursing the lords
Spiky hirsute
Lords the poets' suit
Do describe to shun
Poets from having fun
In their world compelled
Which beggars repel
With thanks to their kin

Exposing their spin.

Change II

Poets love, adore and cherish change
The junky in the streets would he had some change
So is it for the punk
As well as with the drunk
These poor souls would never see its sunrise
And the poet calling for one pays the price
For any such call
Standing him above the head tall;
Yet, change the throne would die for
Change the holy ground would it had four
If poets and people in the streets
See it far from anything coins and sheets
The throne and the mitre would embrace it in their pocket
To wield might and shoot like a rocket.
Toeing political lines one dreamer dreamt of this
And in the streets, all identified as his
For with him, might would visit them thus
And help sweep away obsolescence and its boss
When from the enterprise hurtled in a chide
And with him people were dubbed mad Xerox bona fide.
Given the folks do the desire nurse and see the difference
No care should be ministered the word game reference
And would the first estate put reason to motion
And stop hugging status quo to brandish 'n wield emotion
And with our hearts the People would relish the drink of
change
Were it to come from the streets, the valleys or the
mountain range
Real change the dream
And all would it flows like a stream
Or drop down like some fruits
Off trees with melodious sounds streaming from conduits
Driving fruit flies insane
To leave the place free of pain.

Blood & Fire

My pen wept
And silently waited for the head of this nation
To be swept
And swept away by flood
From the nation,
Its tears and blood,
The blood he has spilled,
The blood my pen did bleed
In stead of the suffering in this nation,
Save the king's
Who misery brings
To deprive them of their own ration.

Like the eagle soaring high
My pen spat fire
To burn the king
In hopes of the day of reckoning
When power will return to the streets
Where it belongs and not on sheets
Altered at the king's guise
For this sleazy disguise.

Today, lamenting over my people's plight
News came to me my country tonight
Bathes in blood and is on fire
And by thoughts of extrication from the quagmire
Carried away, I sat up to do justice
To my people who've only borne injustice.
So, I have to burn at midnight
Its candle before going to bed tonight
And hoping it brightens the warriors' path
For laughs, smiles and jubilation as aftermath
Of a struggle for freedom
Which for years eluded the kingdom.

The Grass and the Beasts of this Earth

Carry their morning
Dew without pain
And quietly sapping
The ground without strain

The soothing green
Grasses in the plain
Must face the beasts' disdain,
For the beasts of this earth as seen

Over the strength impaired
Must have their triumph declared
And at top of voices sing
And treat all others worth nothing

In the fields where they stump
Beating the dew as they would the scum
Yet, the grass roots keep sapping
Like a grassroots' poet tapping

Inspiration from around
With his ears to the ground
Striving to see them survive
Even when they're set on fire live

They their ashes
Like phoenix's crushes
All hopes of never
Seeing them flourish ever

And the beasts must in her dwell
Whether or not they fare well
Living one with another
Always drawn together

Yet, one must dance their triumph
And the other would fight for triumph
In this world of inequity

With grass and poet dreaming of equality

Our Case

Kill our earthly stars.
What will you do to the heavenly ones?
To protect yourself, grease the soldiers' beard.
What shall you do when at your door death knocks?
Bring us the Opposition in a coffin.
But will you let us freely mourn?
You kill our poets.
Do you believe we will bury their writings?
Bury yourself amidst a zillion soldiers.
Haven't you learned from Chinese History?
Like you, in China one did this.
Did he not rot underground?
You sum your world with Law and Order.
Why let lawlessness and disorderliness reign?
You are god to those who buy your favours.
Who or what are you to those you strip of basic rights?
Every night, you go to sleep on a king size bed.
Why not make your heart the size of your bed?
You ruin the nation to live in a mansion.
What space in it or our minds do you occupy?
You've dominated the nation tyrannically.
Shall you ever be the tyrant that kills death?
We thought to rule was to serve.
Why must a tyrant like you be served?
Now, to yourself, you've gathered the nation's wealth?
Won't you give us the right to determine the future of our misery?
You push your tyranny, your greed and grip on power to the last.
Won't you still be proven wrong from beginning and end?
You may never stand in front of any court to plead guilty.
But which other criminal supersedes you?
With your sentence as long as life,
Shall you in your dead bed rule over us?
You may never see this as a case.
But, here, are we not free to rest our case?

Before You Hang Me

Hate or oppress me
Hang or shoot me
Burn or bury me…!

But before this twist
Let me clench my fist
Let me provide a gist:

Let me sing
To the men and their king
A song that like bee sting

Awakes them to the load
Carried by us with a moral code
Reduced like some toad

Cast with a spell
Shut in a well
With no story to tell.

Hearing my song
They shall see what's wrong;
Take the orders then for me to be wrung.

Shooting, hanging, wringing solve not the problem
But attracts a boo for an anthem
Leaving blood, fire and grief as their emblem.

As of stone they have made their hearts
None will ever to them doff their hats
But all will confirm they replicate rats.

Then and only then
Smolder me, not my pen

With flames before I count ten.

Peacefully, I shall die
Heartily, my spirit will fly
Disgracefully, will the king comply.

I shall be death but not gone.
The People shall have, with the king, done
For prising from them their dawn.

Message Bearer to the Monster

Old bottle old beer
We are still and young
And won't cup your beer
Poisonously strong

Crime, your song in rhyme
With which you make merry
That we at our prime
Won't embrace from you pixie

Murder, your act for might
Does your ignominy crown
And we will fight
Till you are down

Police brutality, your shield
Sends reports of many a killing
And against it we stand in the field
Till the harm stops breathing.

Crushing our rights, your daily chore
Supper power support, you've got?
Listen, we are resistant to the core
And will never stoop to be treated like a sot

Your daily delight? A bottle of whisky!
My mind! You won the game?
We identify your voice, husky
And only you will shoulder the blame

Blood spills on our streets, your shame
Flood our towns and make us weep
Yet, with arrogance you sing fame
That is a cheap sweep.

New grave, new baby!
The nation is reborn!
Uplifting hearts happy!
With the monster gone!

Gainsay no true say
That's tribute to the resistance
For having with a thread woven this day
On which we downed the monster with brilliance!

Boxed in a Farm

Forlorn in the field, at one end gazing at the ratoon
The poor little boy had seen, only in his mind, a cartoon.

His seedlings fresh from the nursery in hand
Up he looked at the sun declining west
And reflected on what he thought best
When from his curvature all day he did stand

In himself, the poor little planter
A poet saw, not a potter
As thoughts ran through his head
With the world laughing at him instead

For in the clayey mud he stood
Of which only a pot could turn out good

And with his rattle head ghettoized in a box
Never will he embrace the brains of a fox.
Yet, there hopefully, his rice
He planted and for the next sunrise
Waited. His seeds spread in a kind of order
And he the force of order
Adorning a poetic license
With words here and there to make sense
Just where all see none in the mix
Of clay and that which little fingers transfix

Through her.
In a poem, look not far!
For the poem is its fertilizer
The boy's ratoon and transplants' fertilizer

Need
For feed
As his proem
His liking lit for a Poem.

And that evening greeted the first sketch from his mind
And all the oppression waived, he ne'er was blind!
And he sees, draws and hears the beautiful sunset
And listens to the music from his mind's trumpet.

In poetry, the poor little planter himself found
And cheerful he homeward bound
Freed from the farm box
And away from the predator fox!

Dixeption

Each time I listen to Nature
I hear voices so mature
And looking around, I see an alliance

Nature urges is a mesalliance
I call an attempt to calm my agitated soul
And calm, Nature, I let its course follow.

The Tyrant reigns supreme…
In his delusional scheme
Thinking, over his subjects, dominion

He has, when in death's opinion
He's just another knave
Thinking flirting the best way to behave.

The Tyrant may please himself
And when death shows itself
Might attempt distracting for doing its work

Death shall heed not and mock
The camaraderie tyrants did with him contract
And failed to spell out their aversion for the tract

Now, death at their door, they must go down
Were it in the morning, no waiting for sundown
The time is the time

Even when at the prime
Of life itself, they must go with woe
Having attracted many a foe

Peace with no restrain
Must reign;
A severe blow

Dealing to all tyrants here below
Crushing and undermining Nature and Man
Which all should reprimand.

As I approach my grave

As I approach my grave
Holding firm to my flag of the brave
And seeing all wanting to play save

I, the romantics remember
They would, in their club, have had me member
Not just to swell the number

But to Grace
My place
In the sacred race

Alas! They went
Their wave didn't vent
With the last of them bent

On flagging the metaphysics
With no thoughts of physics,
But the passing time in lyrics

To a container carrying remains
Of what the time harried in his trains
Rather the soul stimulating not just the brains

For this reasoning part dies
While the emotional flies
When the body in the grave lies

To him that approaches his grave

Refusing to be reason's slave
Leaving emotion and fantasy to rave!

The Poet and the Human World

The poet may of the tragic stock be
Never will he of the greedy stock be
He may out of choice a god worship
Never will he cheer the deeds of a warship
Songs calling the downfall of a tyrant he does tune
But dirges to bury the tyrannised his entrails at noon
Spew
For all, not a few!
The flaw of trusting his foible is
The breach of trust from his love, his tragedy is.
A poet is a poet
Human and poet
And a child though
He of mud makes dough,
In pain has one love
In joy has one love
In writing shares either pain and joy
Or both for men with these toy
Espousing the things of this world
Far removed from his world.

To Grace Dethrone

Up there, they always play
We don't as such pray
Here in the house
King there, here mouse
And in the middle
Sounds the fiddle
Invoking Bacchus
Pushing all to bury the curse
But for him in whom euphoria
Dwells in the mind's utopia
And he on this path treaded
And by others discarded
In his flight
Bearing at heart the plight
A pen in hand,
Paper in hand,
With the one on the other birthing
In Euphoria pure king
And not excesses
No one sees
Without the subliminal journey
Embarking
And at the politicking barking
Though all the sucker flea
See
None dares point out
For fear of being wiped out
By the kings' successes
Feeding his excesses
As they erect
The Courts that correct

Mousy conducts
That miss their docks.

The Walls of My Love

The concrete walls of my love
Are steel strong gluing my cove
Unflinching to the flame of enmity that burns
But do embrace a fiery passion that turns
Any one hundred and eighty degrees
With or without degrees
To follow their heart
And on their target land like a dart
To their pounding heart still
Cognisant another heart does theirs steal
For barricaded by these love walls
Not even a shelled volley their love stalls
Stalling the freshness of love
Needing neither perfumes nor a trough
'Coz it is oxygen pure
And does a thirst cure
And like the Spring
Does joy bring.

The Last Word

Politicians use words only to deceive.
Poets use words to enlighten and convince.

Soon after election forgotten are politicians' words.
Long after their death resonate poets' words.

For politicians the word sword is an armament.
For the poets, nothing but an ornament.

For politicians a word is a weapon of mass deception.
And for the poet, it is just a brush for mass decoration

The politicians' mouths like the barrel vomit words to kill
The poets spit words like the dragon spitting fire to still

Driving words to reach the heart like a spear
Or a sword reaching to kill lies politicians tell us here!

Poet's Heart's Desire

Craving and praying for Peace
He does believe in Peace
Not just individual Peace
But world Peace
And wonders how it can be found
Needing no trumpet to sound
Needing no bark from a hound
To leap on board and homeward bound
Finding Peace streaming from conscience
Needing no science
Calling for lots of Patience
But the interment of nascence.
Gently guiding towards her
He shows she is not far
And that like a star
Far from anything scar
She does shine
With rays so fine
Like the sun's twilight's decline
The Heart's desire's holy shrine.

The Grip on our Health

Years now since we had the rain
For years now we've had this pain
When the rain came our way
We sang, rain, rain go away
For we hungered sunshine
Who came and turned us blind
And blind with our minds we see
And would our sight remained at sea
For rain, rain to come again
And not drag our sights down the drain
For we neither love pain
Nor strain
And I would all be pain free
And freely fly like the bee
For freedom is what we all seek
And not oppression of which I am sick
Grip not our health
Poor rain for it brings no wealth.

Rhythm of the Lands

Otherness, the song others sing
Knowing trouble it will bring,
Steals and kills man's greatest desire
With unrest shooting up in a spire
And in a mire left
With no choice of right or left.
Yet, every Nation has a heart
And even those like ragged mat
Trampled upon with great motion
Need rekindling with oration;
Lying on its ground
Listening to its sound
Beat like a heart!
No, it is really a heart!
That of a Nation for its people
Low, low down to earth needing no steeple
But just one thing: an ear
To do just one thing: listen to hear!
Its music, rhythmical
Its rhythm, musical
Where the steeple with its belfry
Blurs minds like clouds do the sky
On her leaving a rumple
With Nations' heart drumming the trouble.

Song Number 13

I listened to the song and knew it wasn't twist
And pondered and pondered as a linguist
And asked a question
Seeking satisfaction:
Bona, the musician's name was
So, good, I did find it was
And in his first name Richard I found rich
And my dead wish all were rich
Yet, in his drumbeat I found
Good and rich exceeding no bound;
Just song number 13
Not Friday the 13
Elatingly rich spiritually
Latinly elating intellectually.

The tropical singer does sing
Quest not to know what he does sing
For the beats of his drum
The heart of this world pump
And feeling the heart beat
A melody sweet like sugar beet
The dancers enthrals
And the heavy footed appals!

Beat drumbeat, pump the heart,
Turn out warmth like the hearth
And off the stage sweep the bald
Seeking rule with their ribald
And let your beat tell me the plight of man
Drained in loving all he can.

Tears for Peace and Love

Passions, humans do express in ways different
Some positions totally indifferent
Some in the aquarium, the gold fish
Freedom deprive and others in their plates relish!

From within my soul I caged a bird
A bird I caged from birth
Making it my everything
When the world turn around to nothing!

Chased out of the window is the dove!
And the tears from my eyes sing for Peace and Love
And query what is to this world left, if the poet
His voice loses and sings not his part in the duet?

Let the tears roll down the cheeks
Let them roll to fill all the creeks
With the poet's natural glove
He wears for mankind to find that grove.
Being all poets let's head for the dove
And bring him home, with our heads up above
Up above the mire of blood they would we drowned
In. Poets do ignominy drag down! Down, down, down!

Dulcet

Like a gentle breeze the music caresses
Human hearts with the softness of fleece
Leaving humans nodding agreeably
Seeing the leaves play the music joyfully
Bringing home the perfumes from lands
Far, far away through which smells to those lands
Transported we are
And thus can see no land is far
For the mind's eye has everything near
And no distant sound away from the ear
And no sweetness of love untasted
Not already tasted
For our everything,
When all is left with nothing
'N by rogues shattered a piece,
Is any dulcet piece.

Travelling on the Spot

Digging and digging they found the rising sun
Through my window I went to the rising sun
On the spot sitting,
Fun loving, fun riding.
The day. Bright and sunny.
And from my brother Sunny
And Queen Irene
Comes a ring
That spurns such a laugh
That for centuries none ever did have;
Thinking myself a poet
These two point out as would any poet
This rare gem with which we are gifted:
Travelling the world round on the spot seated
With our vocabulary knowing no take off
And never in our journey walking off
And days and days after, I still hear the French
Sweet, smooth and caressing with no cheesy stench:
"Seul homme du monde habileté
A voyager sans jamais décoller."
And it sparked and still does laugh

Laugh, laugh

As S & I my day brightened
The laughs my days lengthened
And true to my poetic vocation
Never shall I take off for vacation
To feast my eyes on things I freely see
Having no need to voyage across the sea.
Sunny keep shining and brightening
So in our circle we won't break the ring.

Hearing The Voiceless

In spite of this gripping quiet and blackness surrounding,
This special melodic, rhythmical sound emerging from
within
Defies human description and scrutiny
And hints on the overwhelming importance
The overwhelming importance
Of the connection
The connection
Of the Inner Voice
And the voiceless, their voice
Within telling their travail,
Hopes and aspirations shall prevail
In the like this melody is savoured
And thankfully hearing this sound I am favoured!

TRANSPARENCY

White
Paper sheet
As you gave opaque pen
One kiss
Worse than
Night
Fall
Your plain's defined
None dreams a grain
Nor loss again
Impregnated ye carry
Words
To turn out
Machine gun-like, pout
Horror for Head
And
Lullaby for the un
I beam with joy
Like a loving guy
Who gleams his gun
To the head pointed;
With them brush in hand
To painting
The guy subversive king.

May Be In A Dream

I don't think
I don't drink
Just about to pen opposites
Whence Walcott hurtled in with "Negatives"
I stammered
With his voicing in them hit – la!
He and him are down in History
And we have at least a story;
The one in the military
The other in the literary
And I bow to the literate,
His militancy not the military illiterate
Against literacy
Driving him with arms crazy
Giving an amount of nous
To name them …. God knows!
Both militate
One destroys, the other creates.

THE SEINE BY NIGHT
[*A Regular Visitor P(un)der(s)*]

Plodding down
Pondering dawn,
Halt or glide smoothly
Leaving the homeless lonely?
Oh, Liberty!
Sweet liberty!
Were you not Faustus'
Queen in parade
Magicking away in raid
In maze letting us
No, the profane
Would, France had another fame
And she is your country
Country of Liberty
And to you married
When she in her have you buried
And I see you in parade
Like the French military in parade
To give true meaning to come
To that which you have become
And I continue my song
When liberty is unsung
       Oh,   Freedom
             Freedom
             Freedom
       Oh,   Freedom fighters
May you be born again for us
To have eighty-nine more years
And sing thy sweet name
With all the joys and no pain
And be glad you live Liberty!
             And that you are not a scarce commodity!

CARTRIDGES

Papers' filigrees
From my nip trickling
Hail filibuster;
Were silence golden
To sleep sea would
                        Plop
Words cajoling ears,
Caressing hearts,
                Embroidering desires'
        Quest
    To ignite conquest….
Bleeding from black over white.

The Seer

He needs no beer
For he is a seer
And might look and act like a sheep
But is he who never goes to sleep
And knows no difference between
The passing and passed time twin
Brothers. Bridging the gap for workman,
Giving a good shake to the foreman,
Mastering the here and now,
Mastering the hereafter
And constantly tuned to midnight
For the spirit to come spark his light
To pierce through even the thickest cloud
And fill with grout not doubt
The shaky foundations
On which sit many nations
In a world so worldless
With human caring less
For the advent of the universe
And even more so for rhymed or unrhymed verse.
Yet,
Yes!
In his blood
In his thoughts
In his walks
In his rest
At his best
And even in his snooze
With some booze
He handles the torch
That will never scorch
But with it streams his hopeful ray
Beyond humanity growing grey.
And always on the path of the inner light finds his strength
Keenly listening to the inner voice and at length
Translating these words onto paper
For people to savour in theatres before dinner.

Heart and tongue

       The poet is the eye!
       The poet is the ear!
       The poet is the nose!
       The poet is the tongue!
       The poet is the heart!
       The poet is the sixth, seventh, eighth, and ninth senses!
       That of the suffering poor!

Need he the eyes to see the entrails of their suffering?
Need he the ear to hear their lamentations and growling?
Need he a nose to smell the stench of the political mishmash?
Certainly not. but he sure does a heart need for those in the marsh
Abandoned for in his heart, he has eyes, ears, and nose planted
And sure he does for the voiceless need one articulated
Tongue
That resonates and like a gong
To bring them together
Using the sixth, seventh, eighth, and ninth senses better.

The Transporter

The train of life stops here
The train of life goes there
Stop here or go there brings with it
Some memory, sad or joyous be it.

The transporter carries with him hope
But dashes it soon down the slope
Putting on the faces of many a smile
And in the end, pushing them to sigh.

Having brought joys and hopes at my conception
And being here in this situation,
One ask when again will the train stop here
And were one to know, would that be fair?

Alas! He will come with his cold, cold hands
And force hair to stand in strands
For life will be forever still were this not the case
And so this train, we can't chase.

Welcome the train of joy,
Unwelcome the train that destroy,
Recycling life being his mission
For which he needs no human permission.

Tell me when the train comes in today,
I will tell you what all will say:
Some will the mystery of creation celebrate
And some will that same mystery ending the voyage hate.

Either way, things are never the same.
The welcoming party scores a win in the game
And the farewell bidding party will endorse
A great loss carted home by a horse!

So does the train from door to door go round
And so is the fate of Man bound
Over the moon in happiness
And down, down under in sadness

When this happens we can't help but ask
Why we can't chop him with an axe.
But the clever and invisible train
Has no business with enduring pain.

Where we differ.

To right the wrong
For rights we fight
And they fight for might
To show they're strong.

To please the mind we sing
And soothe the soul
And they care less for any poor soul
And to rabble to rouse mankind, their thing.

To have people dance
And share their joy we stand
And they would all like flies were on sand
For them to cast a mocking glance.

We would the earth of milk and honey
Flow
And they would a blow
On its face slap with money.

The poor we cherish
And provide for
These they would for
Their might die in a ditch.

To give a piece of cake
And help all find some peace
We would and they would all went apiece
And wished all at their sight quake.

We stand never, never to laugh,
Laugh at any for being indigent
Here, they find a spicy ingredient
To haughtily scuff.

We, our joy, derive from simplicity,
Gentleness, kindness and thoughtfulness
They're quick to get theirs from madness birthing sadness
And would gladly encourage a cult of personality

Where we vouch for moderation as fundamental
And would it the pillar on which leans our ism
Without duplicity they embrace extremism
And vouch it is the most essential.

When humanity against itself turn
We strife to put on her face, a smile
They would they told the world we're senile
And would in turn send us to the journey of no return.

Where we burn with zeal
And would freedom reign
They would the nation their domain
And with us they'd make their meal of veal

Here we would you choose
And freedom advocate
And they would they dictate
And will never let you loose

After you've finished reading these lines
You could choose where to belong
And we would tell you it won't be long
Before they put you behind enemy lines.

This is how we differ
For neither you nor I can refute
Though we all know the flute
Can tune our world finer!

The Scum B…!

In the years of yore we had commandments
Our visitors assumed in the dark we lived our moments
And thought it wise to sum theirs in just ten
And believed us ignorant for we wrote not with a pen

Yet, like cats we lived in the dark by them
With sight and insight that of gem
They were not made
And away stayed from their bait

In perfect harmony living with our environment
And embracing and turning her virescent
With non-violence our norm dogmatized
By their obsolescence destabilized

And not blind saw we them back all in this good book
And not blind still, noted we, them of the stock of crook
Readily turning forebears into bones
And did these use as building stones

Having the foundation with their bones laid
And with the sweat and blood of the old their fortune
made
And we patiently their good sense questioned
And the defenders wouldn't the like be mentioned

Peering through the soil we find it is rich in nitrate
And looking around, we see so much hatred
And now we understand the nitrate from sweat came
The sweat and blood of forebears their badge of shame

The Sweat and the Blood fed crops on the land
That on riches did them land
And we the stain that be on their robes
Visible and hanging the like of lobes

Our lives unspiced with such condiments
As would the commandments
Not to steal from thy neighbour
Sing of our travail and labour

Showing its hump the like of a whale
Just as on their coasts, did the ships with human bale
Legating the indelible scar
That forever blackens the star

Yet, we being true warriors, our personal history cancel
And would the victors' be revisited in council
For true love, peace and harmony to reign
With crops neither by blood nor sweat fed but by rain.

Haunting Past

These trees on this land have fed for generations
And their leaves would not negate adorations
Were it to revert to the darker side of the history
And face up to the engendered misery

Reparation is the word most did and do fear
And stolen wealth, the dress they did and do wear
They might not have been the thieves themselves
But did inherit all the thieves had on their shelves.

If legating the ignominy of a hangman
Haunts you, then seek to be a best man
To him that a bride waits down the aisle as a groom
To bury the haunting shadow to be of gloom

And many a man feeding on the dregs of shame
And attempting to stay free of blame and claim
Would refuse to acknowledge
The disinherited sitting on society's edge

And more, they who inherit from highway
Men refute they never did rob on the highway;
Denial none needs
But admittance of ancestral deeds

And if not, possible return of stolen goods
When on their shoulders deeds of yore be their roods
And only restoration and reparation
Would efface History

Negating responsibility for parents past
Brings home rejection of inheritance at last
So, the claims laid
For misdeeds need be paid.

Hands and Heart

With both hands and heart stretched out,
Life you say is complex,
My vision you style simplistic!
Yet, I am glad!
                      Glad to have known
                                            U

                  A second
Glad to be   Abel,
      To handle a pencil,
      To scribble Poe-
                        [Try]
And all reckon I did try
And with no eyes
My heart bleeds tears
With both hands and heart still stretched out!

Beyond Desire

In you, my dove I did find
And to you myself I would bind
Seeing you fly away
Over and above a Jay
Flying like the smoke you puff away,
My dove
        My luv
              I would…
I would make you…!
           No! How can I?
I see
I see you are….
Yes! No doubts, far, far above
Above Nerval's "Aurelia"
And like Gerald
How can I dine?
I am mad….
Mad?
Yes!
In   El Oh! Vee Ee!
One for U
        Refuge of my senses,
One for me,
The quintessence
Of that honey bee U tee which enlivens
Many a manly poet to hug his pen
And caress his sheets
In search of you
Making a glimpse of you
Rarity number one
Where my innermost would you my number one…!

Fool Not Thyself

Live thy truth overtly
And only then can life wholly
Be! When of secrets thou thy life
Make, thou trickest none
But the mass thou hast known
All thy life!
        Live a life
                  And let the life
With and in thee
                    Live…!

Tickle Their Minds

Tickle their minds for just one minute
Setting them to realms of the spirit
And let thy madding music
The music that sooths them mystic
And thy shadow a perfect conduit

A perfect one for a frantic quest
For that which intrigues all west
Making for them a nest
In earnest
They all desire for their rest…!

WHAT DOES IT MATTER?

What does it matter
Taking me for the shadow of matter
Or myself
When in life no elf
Came to show the world that which I am:
A heart that would never pick up an arm?
How does it change the order,
The order of things past, present or
Even the advent of the universe
Penning a verse?
What & where is life?
Is it this stupid jive?
Is it shitty,
Iffy
?

Hic et nunc,
Life is sapid!
And we must sip it!
And we must zip it!
And that's life
For which all should strife!

Like all the others
We are having a lay over
With no thoughts
Of a hang over
Come tomorrow
But of a stronger marrow
And the clock ticks
Like drips from licks
And all we aspire
Discarding the mire
Is none but a better
Greasy morrow with butter
To butter whose bread,
When the dire need for children is seen as a threat?

STRONG, STRONG WEAK

Too strong at picking up a gun
And weak, weak, weak at lifting a pen
He like a pendulum swings his forte
And points him at poor little weak Billy
Poor little weak Billy from the foothill
That hosts the colourful anthill
Which in his youth led and won
Him wars against uphill Bully the gun
Carrier.

Too strong, strong at picking up a pen
And uphill Bully only see in him
Nothing but Job
                    Grabber
                         Job
                           Reincarnated!

Commemoration

Looking at clouds
Cluster in moulds
And sail in sky
Grooms brain spy
To image
Man's voyage
Along whose courses
He fight for causes
To destinations
Unknown with no solutions
To his utter bewilderment
Crystallising the quest for the fate of great men
Who sojourned
And journeyed along
Unnoticed to macrocosm
But to microcosm;
Should one think and know

One unknow_
Able, mystery will become
Placeless in every lexicon…
You may ask why
Such silly thought…? Why?
Simple my response:
Ages before I was,
By the first war
Who shook the world
My sun rose,
By the third's eve, off he dosed.
None saw the sunshine,
I felt it's warmth in mind.
And same date
As today, with no date,
News came my key was lost.
It was not dusk
With abandon, I
Pondered why…!
The absence,
A tree's that in essence,
Constitutes in itself
A forest and falls off.
Walking pass through,
I realised 'twas true
All left was artificial
And nothing natural;
None ever laughed again
But showed their teeth, the laughter, maimed.
Should your sun preciously set,
May I ask… my thought
That stupid
Or the journey worth starting?
It marked not the end of things
Though overturned many things:
Solitude ignited same Friday
And today, Tuesday
Would preciously mark own end
Before my journey's end
For people to look at Biography
Cautioning peace
In Peace
Nursing the import of History.

The Messenger

Little bee
When thou buzz
Would thou
In the ears
Of the dead;

Wake them from sleep
To come tell us
Of our Mothers:

Were they these
Buzzards in skirts?

And would for them
Little bee drive them

With thy magic
                    Music
Take them away from the weak;

These weak preys
With graceless praise
Warranting buzzards' life

As they drop out of life

Buzz thy music
Till they top the peak!
Little,
Little Bee !

I WONDER

Why not ten poems
A day in Paris?
Was the interrogation!
I would I could fifty
In an hour
                                        Were I not to spend
That running to catch
                        The bus
The subway
                                        For my job
The course
                        And grab a sandwich
                                        For a bite…!!
                So goes life in Paris
And so are the fifty
                                        Per hour poems gone!
                Poems I would
Twelve hundred have done
                        A day
                Lie buried in this CT
        Not the woods in her backyard of yesteryears
                Up the Hills of Montmorency
                Where centuries ago
                        Rousseau
Birthed the *Contract*
That engineered the Revolution
That killed the *Contract*

                                        At full revolution
                        Leaving the streets of Paris
                                With poems littered
The range of which stretch so far to the grange:
        From the gloomy frown in the subway
                To the half gloomy grin on the passage way
                        Such dazzles as would revive Chaucer's May

Stun as to   why   all Parisians aren't poets…!

68

The Voice Of A Resting Soul

When I accepted death my son
You were too poor son
Too poor to offer a drink
Those who clustered around the thing
I'd become; one for the deeps
Or one ready to sail in the sea like ships!
You placed in my hands
To take down to my New Hammock
Two sheets with your mind
In them reading that hyper lucidity
Which stopped people from straining
For my parting after my part playing
And leaving for the young theirs
And I did then acknowledge
Taking cognizance and full knowledge
Of thy plainness of heart
Of the love you did all thy
Span in mine conceal
To give you nothing but this seal
And through it you shall yourself
Humble till the day the self
Gets much of that world and say:
"For that I did enjoy and (h)ate, I must pay."

I loved telling you stories
You loved them and read histories
Of this land to which I now belong
From the time church bells tolled: "ding dong"
Inviting me to saying, in spite of your wishes, "quit"
And you did respond with a saucy word: "shit"
Before admitting good believers (Christians)
Must their mouth shot, maintain
That silence needed by a sleeping man
Especially one like me, in his eternal sleep found!
Taking along my tongue of a teller
I leave you a pen and the soul for a thinker

To set the brains and thoughts
Of gods in Ivory Towers
Flying above like clouds.

Mark! Humble
Your humble self; fish no trouble
Till you your invitation accept
For people to chant you your excerpts
As lullaby
For you are gone by
You shall love
And love
And love your mission
Without concealing your passion
For penning panegyrics
Which like aesthetics
Multiply beauty
Which with its lovely
Caresses smoothens the gentle passing
Like that song we chanted marching
Down the street!

In Search For It

Just a blank sheet of paper
It was never taught, my clock.
Green was its music
For its sake, my clock
The pendulum music
Played better.
Its own sound unforgotten,
Dancing but the pendulum tune.

Turning, search I it in the sheets.
Yet, coming it is never.
Return to myself will tarnish all
But Helens say, "return to yourself, farm it ever."
In the cave's under walls
                    Of what use is it?
Wisdom runs towards our roost.
Chased, hunted and hunting we it find most…!

Biography

This child that was
The man that is
The scriber that will be
The tomorrow's laureate
Looked into the childhood world
The world of adulthood
With surprise and hope
All brought to pass in futility
Through K'cracy;
The turbulence of trees
In the storm
Summarizing life
In which all we need is
Pray in peace
For peace
And if neither can,
Do one for another !

Mitigation (*Plea by a marooned Pen*).

Blessed Poet
Spare that soul
Whose ignorance
In the gutter
Me sent idling,
That rich poor soul !

        Ye rescued me
        And with me
        Bury him not
        Nor in pen, put
        Him not like
        Would gaolers......

    With thee, in sooth
    Would, I pen poems
    Slaying not
    That poor rich!

Creator poet,
I acknowledge
Thee creator;
For that wisdom,
Work up minds
Pensively fine!

The Dirge

The child I was, heard one chanted.
Its thrill to my father I repeated.
Hailed him its nicety,
Frowned he at my naivety
And his face wrinkled for my poor timing
And my mouth hurried to question:
Why? "You shall know!" did
My mouth seal
And today I would I sing
One
On seeing autocracy buried;
His spectre like my late father's
Hushed me for my trembling mouth
To sing autocracy is there
And not autocracy is dead,
This, his expectation from song-makers;
Panegyric, his gluing sticker.

Autobiography

Mutism,
My garb
All my life,
Wore out
For me to shout:

'I am'

But my inner man,

My brother
Glimpse in me
In this century
Of the Isms

A drum beater.

Socrates' me
Should be the most dreaded
Yet, my palms' blisters,
My drums' sounds
And the souls pleasure
Maintain SIMA's face....

Urbane Urchin

Mosquitoes' mutiny
A song so tiny
Like a new born child
With no dour print of chide
But admiration
Causing no motion
Though it trekked, no groped
Through the uric road
Prickling throats for a toast
As parents of the dolt boast,
Till in action, his sting
Clutches them to spring
With cacophonic sighs
For noosing heads in melodious sound;
Blinked. From their thighs,
To his knees fell on the ground….

Optimists

With gloom
The only bloom
Keep this broom
As a groom
Wearing a smile
To screen the pile
That makes the pyre
For faithfuls to cluster round, with a lyre
Playing to uplift hearts
Musing "all was not hard."
Though her face was all warts
Burying her smile in a ward.

Darkness must not rule.
The West, sun's grave should.
Keep ye this basic truth,

With thou,
Quest only the upper part
With its affluence
Not the lower with all scarce
Even when thou art there
Dream and claim thou were elsewhere
And thou would be, with a panegyric, lauded
Like god of good humour
Though thou seest grievously no armour;
Such, thou art the good sample optimist,
Yet, thy shadow follows and persists
And thou shall forever insist
O, optimists
Plod along the mist....

The Triad

Whenever death plugs off some feathers
From the wings of life, even fathers
Fall their heads and cry
And the poet will hurry to their tears dry

When life makes a mockery of man
And he contemplates life with a reprimand
The poet dashes forward with words of wisdom
To remind man of the solace of the other kingdom

Death, Life and the Poet
A triad make
Death and Life two sides of a coin make
And the coin owned by the poet

Whose chimes in life echo his death
And so does his death in this life mark his birth!
The one recalls the world treating him like dross
And the other brings home to bear a great loss

Of one so lucid
And able to taste the insipid
Where all found a great taste
And above all could gold get from waste

And himself, treated like it
And with courage braved it
To recount the uselessness of all fight
By embracing and marrying flight

When others need a plane
To fly to Cervantes' Spain
He on the spot goes the world round
Like a child on merry-go-round

And round, life is a cycle
And round in a circle
Humans dance to a maddened tune
Except the poet who unearths the dune

Letting no pen lie
And using it to spew the truth till we die
And letting the dove bring home the Olive
                  Branch, accomplishing why poets live.

The Great Journey

Getting ready for the homeward journey
Let's all remember life's as sweet as honey
And our ultimate end money can't buy
And when he shows up we must bid goodbye

X would he could change
His fate with a challenge
To the inscription in the book of destiny
By asking: "… why hast thou forsaken me?"

When my time comes and I bid farewell
To all the earthly tidings I enjoyed well
Let me go with memories so joyful
And let not your tears fill my grave full.

Here I know no grief
After a life not so brief
Though with me carrying one regret
I would in this advent all forget;

The lines of the muse's visitations
I did forfeit for relaxations
And those poems never born
Accounts for the 'gret I borne!

Those unborn lines are written in the book of destiny
As those never to make the journey
To you. So, why make a fuss
For what steals nothing off your purse?

Smile! Laugh and jolly make
As you for my birthdays enjoyed the cake
And celebrating all these years my birth
Must have tickled minds for my death.

So, let me in this grave of mine lie
And remember true poets never die
Were all to remain faithful
That which from you your poet pull

Home to rest
And at worst putting you to test
My parting will from you welcome a chance
And read not you in it any mischance.

Adieu!
Adieu!
And to the crown be glory
For with it there is no history.

Thinking Freedom

When birds fly 'coz they're free
What a delight to see?
When away from the hunter flying,
How heart wrenching?

Like freedom birds flying, poets
Come up with the loveliest duets
But the audience so embroiled,
Embroiled in the daily toil
By one class imposed
Is hardly disposed
To enjoying this gift
Of the Heart
Intended to lift
Up their heart.

Freedom poets, keep the tune alive
For the toil is the fuel of your life
Were it to be the path to your grave;
How else can we know you're grave?

The Pungent Staple

Stumbling here and there on Chaucer's godly apple
            I would none made it their staple
      For, this has pushed my people to grub
         'Coz National cash crop
                Reliance does corrupt
And all including the bodiless head want it abrupt
And angry Jack hearing his time was up
Delightfully, after breakfast, gave up,
Giving up the ghost
To follow the path laid by his host;
        He lay down and with satisfaction
Thanked the host for guiding him to this law abiding nation
And seeing others fuss about this shift
I could not but hail the lift
            To this kingdom of believers' aspiration
         Giving me this inspiration
       To doff me hat to a hero so rare
To have embraced the icy coldness of the hereafter without fear
And I wish I owned a gun
To salute him for having gone,
            Doing this with a pen
And far from that nation, away I stay from the pen
          And pray in the freeze, Jack
        His revulsion intones like a lark
        And melodiously feeds our ears
So my people can take up to stamping out the sears.

Help for the President

Going to war with the courage of a lion,
Building a wall of opposition around this nation
In which blind greed and distemper
Has so affected that national father
Driving him into a mad rage
To turning against his own page
And subjects, he with his hands
Shreds them in strands
Setting in fear
As a mask to his rear.

Mr President needs help not a spear
And if so, it would be that which poets use to sear
And stain mark a paper
To bring about the deeper
Cleansing needed by any mad father of a nation
Whose aspiration is rule for a generation.

On the Coming Time

Whirling time in the hope away it flies
The gap closes into adulthood and it multiplies
Time passed never went anywhere
The time to come is always there
Just as dead men never went anywhere.
They have always been here.
Death and dying
Life and living
Their grip on man has
Just as man his on them has
When man gets the best of life
At his death the best of man's life
Join the pages of history
Unfolding a mystery,
One to be told
Or left in the cold….

Life and living
Rhymes with Death and dying
For life will no longer be life
Were men to slay the transition to eternal life.

And were man's plight to live and die
Let me have that piece of pie,
And give me it with a smile
When readying the cremation under the pile
Or when digging me grave
Tell the knave the story of a brave.

The wealth of Clouds' Voyage
(Baby Understanding)

Looking up in the sky
A baby greeted the clouds voyaging high
And having no doubts,
He wished to confirm his thoughts
Of a journey to the end of the world,
A beautiful journey striking the chord,
The chord of a lyre
Stringing against the big fat liar
And a reminder of the order of things
That the movement of the clouds brings
And recalling the experiences of the Little Prince,
His Knowledge let him not prentice
In the school of adult babble
Where, with meanings, he will be left to dabble.
In quest of man's creativity,
In vain, he helpfully recalls man his nativity
And wondered how these happen
And whether it would, were man to keep pushing his pen.

ANIMISTS 2 PRAY!

Perch not on that dome
Bird of Wisdom
Bird of Freedom;
Fly to our kingdom….
Come along with a scone….

Come, Come dry our watery

Mouths and make starry
The bleak sombre scary
Sky whose extraordinary

Wisdom generates misery…!

Leave us not behind

Leave none in a bind

And by the hand take the blind

And translate the wicked kind

With all on the path of thy mind!

A
N
D

Let
It
Be
!

LET US DREAM

Be it Spring, Summer,
Autumn or Winter,
The rainy or the dry seasons
Allow these images colouring your screens
Flocking in from the Near East,
The Far East,
Africa and beyond
Resurrect a conundrum
In the child in you to questing

What if…!

We took our comedy away
Far, far away
From Dante's
Making her humane
Having humans with humans
Playing
Not with each other's sentiments
Nor with one and others' life,
Will tragedy then
Not be divine…?

Dream on child…!

The Poets' See, Saw

Poets delight not in seesaw
But all pains they see they saw
The only way to our society keep sane
In this world where the drive is gloriously vain
Quest for an illusion not concrete happiness
Pricking life like a thorn to turn to nothingness,
Nothingness for the head that rules
Ruthlessly thinking we were fools
When our dreams of happiness they should grace
So we shall happily follow their trace
Yet, poets must the pains see and saw
Not merry make on a seesaw.

Word Power: Dilly

Wielding his power, the ignorant head would spue
Volleys out of the cannons and in his thinking knew
They would command great respect hither
And not into abhorrence slither
And would they supersede
Poets' simpler words that recede
Into the depths of human emotion
And always tickle the imagination
Spurring not only war, fright and sadness
But Peace, Love and Happiness,
Flowing from the milky river whose spring
Is the poets' Heart making all smiling
'N keeping the word alive and weighting it over
The volleys in slumber.